AF442166

WILDLIFE IN LAKES & PONDS FOR KIDS
(Aquatic & Marine Life)
2nd Grade Science Edition Vol 5

SPEEDY
PUBLISHING

Speedy Publishing LLC
40 E. Main St. #1156
Newark, DE 19711
www.speedypublishing.com

Copyright 2015

All Rights reserved. No part of this book may be reproduced or used in any way or form or by any means whether electronic or mechanical, this means that you cannot record or photocopy any material ideas or tips that are provided in this book

A lake is a large body of fresh water. Lakes can range in size from small ponds to huge bodies of water.

The sturgeon has been referred to as primitive fish because their features have stayed little changed since their earliest fossil record.

Sturgeon range from subtropical to subarctic waters in North America and Eurasia.

Shrimps are perhaps the most widely known marine crustacea.

Shrimp are widespread and abundant. They can be found feeding near the seafloor on most coasts and estuaries, as well as in lakes.

Crayfish are freshwater crustaceans resembling small lobsters. Crayfish feed on living and dead animals and plants.

Crayfish appear in many different colors, with red crayfish usually being the most common.

Alligator gar is the largest of the freshwater gars. The freshwater gars are part of an ancient family of predatory fish.

Alligator gars inhabit a wide variety of aquatic habitats, but most are found in the Southern United States in reservoirs and lakes.

The common snapping turtle is a large freshwater turtle. Snapping turtles are solitary, which means that they live alone.

The common snapping turtle is noted for its combative disposition when out of the water with its powerful beak-like jaws, and highly mobile head and neck.

The axolotl is colloquially known as a "walking fish". The axolotl is only native to Lake Xochimilco and Lake Chalco in central Mexico.

Axolotl can reach the size of up to 12 inches in the length and the weight of up to 8 pounds.

The sunfish
are native
only to North
America.
They prefer
slow moving
water such as
lakes, or slow
moving rivers.

The male
of most
species builds
a nest by
hollowing out
a depression
using his tail,
then guards
the eggs.

A tadpole is the larval stage in the life cycle of an amphibian, particularly that of a frog.

Most types of
tadpole eat
only plants.
Some types
of tadpole
eat plants
and animals.

A newt is
a type of
salamander.
This mainly
solitary
animal
is found
throughout
Asia, Europe
and North
America.

Adult newts have lizard-like bodies and may be either fully aquatic, living permanently in the water.

Visit

BABY PROFESSOR
EDUCATION KIDS

www.BabyProfessorBooks.com
to download Free Baby Professor eBooks
and view our catalog of new and exciting
Children's Books

www.ingramcontent.com/pod-product-compliance
Lightning Source LLC
Chambersburg PA
CBHW081149180726
48003CB00026B/3038